Decision Analysis
In Projects

Library of Congress Cataloging-in-Publication Data

Schuyler, John, 1950–
    Decision analysis in projects / by John Schuyler.
      p.   cm.
    Includes bibliographical references and index
    ISBN 1-880410-39-7 (pbk.)
    1. Industrial project management—Decision making — Statistical
methods.   2. Statistical decision.   I. Title.
HD69.P75S38 1996
658.4'04–dc20

96–34113
CIP

BOOK TEAM
Editor-in-Chief: James S. Pennypacker
Editor, Book Division/Production Coordinator: Mark Parker
Graphic Designer: Michelle Owen
Acquisitions Editor: Bobby R. Hensley
Associate Editor: Sandy Jenkins
Proofreader: Ann Wright

PMI books are available at special quantity discounts to use as premiums
and sales promotions, or for use in corporate training programs. For more
information, please write to the Business Manager, PMI Communications, 40
Colonial Square, Sylva, North Carolina 28779 USA. Or contact your local
bookstore.

The paper used in this book complies with the Permanent Paper Standard
issued by the National Information Standards Organization (Z39.48–1984).

10 9 8 7 6 5 4 3 2 1

Contents

List of Tables

Preface

IS THERE ANYTHING MORE IMPORTANT to the success of a project than making good decisions? This skill is certainly near the top of the list, yet few of us have had formal training in decision making. Decision analysis is a discipline that helps people choose wisely under conditions of uncertainty. This book introduces decision analysis applied to project management.

We are seeing increasing interest in probabilistic techniques in all types of evaluation. Shorter business cycles and ever greater competition are *demanding better resource management.* Fortunately, people are learning more about value creation and how to work with uncertainty. New and evolving project management software provides help in assessing and managing risks and opportunities.

This book collects a series of twelve articles from *PM Network*, the professional magazine of the Project Management Institute (PMI). In mid-1992, I was invited to contribute an installment to a decision analysis series. The one article gave way to three installments, which eventually led to the series.

This was not a solo effort. Considerable credit belongs to Dr. Francis M. Webster, PMI's Editor-in-Chief (1987-1994) who guided the first eight installments. Fran kept me focused on project management when I would occasionally revert to my roots, project evaluation. His passion for the project management discipline and depth of knowledge made each piece robust and lucid.

James Pennypacker joined PMI Publications as Editor-in-Chief in the fall of 1994. Jim skillfully oversaw the last four installments as well as the manuscript for this book. It has and continues to be a pleasure working with Jim and the staff of PMI Publications, especially Mark Parker, the lead editor of this book.

PMI has another risk management book: *Project and Program Risk Management: A Guide to Managing Project Risks and Opportunities* edited by R. Max Wideman. This book provides a different, more managerial, perspective about the craft of project management and risks. I believe the two books compliment one another nicely.

The *PM Network* series and this book have been an enjoyable undertaking. And I'm proud of making a contribution to "advancing the state-of-the-art" of project management practice.

Although the probability concepts are well-established, our knowledge of how to apply them continuously evolves. PMI and I will be grateful for your comments and suggestions that will aid in a future revision of this book.

John R. Schuyler
Aurora, Colorado

Please direct comments or inquires to:

John R. Schuyler
c/o Project Management Institute
Publications Division
40 Colonial Square
Sylva, NC 28779 USA

Chapter One

Expected Value: The Cornerstone

Probability is the language of uncertainty. Fortunately, a few basic concepts in probability and statistics go a long way toward making better decisions. This chapter introduces the terminology and a few important concepts.

Introduction

Decision analysis, sometimes called risk analysis, is the discipline for helping decision makers choose wisely under conditions of uncertainty. The techniques are **applicable to all types of project decisions** and valuations. Committing to fund a project does not end the decision making, for decisions continue to be made throughout project life cycle. The quality of these decisions impacts cost, schedule, and performance.

This book explores the approach and principal techniques of decision analysis. These methods explicitly recognize uncertainties in project forecasts. This analysis technology, on the leading edge in the 1970s and earlier, is headed toward becoming mainstream practice. The methodology is proven, accessible, and—I hope you'll agree— easily understood.

Decision analysis provides the only logical, consistent way to incorporate judgments about risks and uncertainties into an analysis. When uncertainties are significant, these techniques are the best route toward credible project decisions.

Goals of Credible Analysis

Your job may involve estimating project or activity costs. How would you evaluate the quality of your estimates? Most forecast users will recognize two principal desirable characteristics:
- **Objectivity:** Lack of bias. On average, over a number of projects, estimates proving neither too high nor too low on average.
- **Precision:** Reasonable closeness of a set of values, minimizing random "noise" in the estimates.

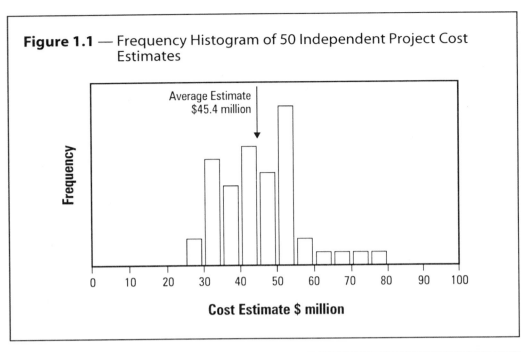

Figure 1.1 — Frequency Histogram of 50 Independent Project Cost Estimates

Average Estimate $45.4 million

Frequency

Cost Estimate $ million

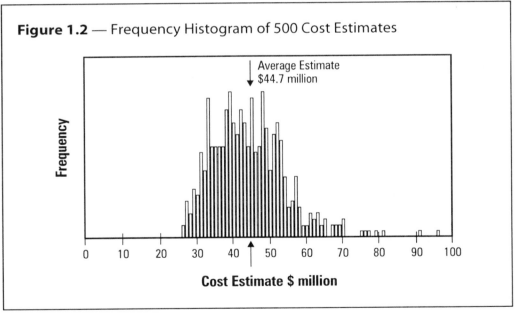

Figure 1.2 — Frequency Histogram of 500 Cost Estimates

Average Estimate $44.7 million

Frequency

Cost Estimate $ million

Forecast accuracy is a composite of low bias and high precision. *Objectivity*—lack of bias—tells us about the estimate quality regarding where the estimate distribution is located on the measurement scale (balance about the true value), and precision tells us about *how values are dispersed* through their central location.

Expected Value: The Cornerstone

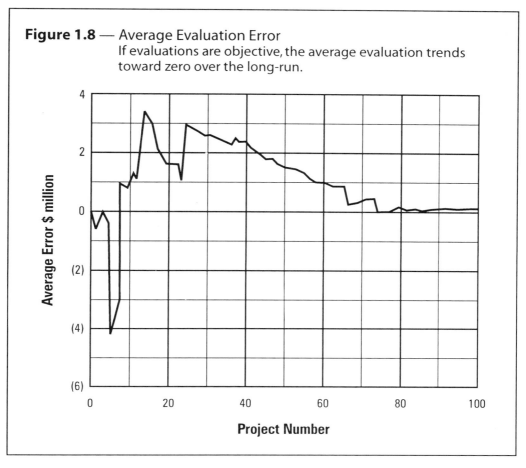

Figure 1.8 — Average Evaluation Error
If evaluations are objective, the average evaluation trends toward zero over the long-run.

This curve, or its cumulative equivalent, expresses the Material Cost assessment. The distribution can be obtained from subjective judgment, comparable historical data, modeling, mathematical formulation, or other means. Regardless of how it comes about, the probability distribution fully discloses one's judgment about the project variable.

Converts to a Single Value

What number should be provided if the client insists on a single value estimate instead of a distribution? The **best point estimate is the expected value**, because it is objective. In the Material Cost case of Figure 1.9, a $2.4 million cost estimate would be provided for the single point forecast.

One would be confident that:
- Performing many similar projects would result in an average Material Cost of approximately $2.4 million.
- Over the long run, the average estimate error will approach zero.

Figure 1.9 — Triangle Probability Distribution Expressing a Judgment About Material Cost Uncertainty

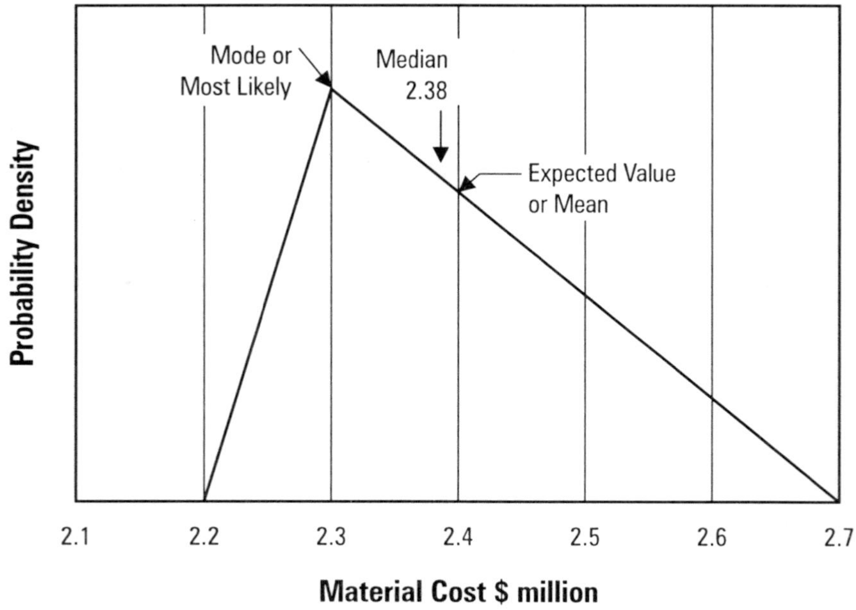

Note that forecasts that use the *most likely* (peak) or *median* (50 percent probability) points would result in a systematic bias in understating Material Cost.

Calculating Expected Value

There are several ways to calculate the expected value of a probability distribution. If the distribution is expressed as a mathematical formula, one might be able to solve the integral equation

$$\text{Expected value} = EV = \int_{all\ x} x\ p(x)dx$$

where x is the value of concern and p(x) is the probability density function of x. For a discrete distribution, EV is the sum of the probabilities times the outcome values:

$$EV = \sum_{i=1}^{n} x_i\ p(x_i)$$

where x_i are the outcome values, and $p(x_i)$ are the probabilities of these outcomes.

For input distributions, expected values can be obtained by numeric integration or graphical methods. We usually calculate the

Table 2.1 — Delay Days Given Activity A15 is Critical.

Delay	Medium Crane		Large Crane	
	Probability	Delay Days	Probability	Delay Days
Long	.2	10	.2	3
Medium	.5	5	.5	2
Short	.3	2	.3	1

This situation can be analyzed with either a payoff table or a decision tree.

If the project goes as planned, activity A15 does not delay the overall completion time. That is, A15 is not on the *critical path* with crane size affecting the project's duration. (Critical path is discussed briefly in Chapter 6). A conventional project analysis sees no benefit of greater crane capacity on the project completion time. In fact, the Large Crane is inferior because of its higher cost.

However, a probabilistic project model (discussed in Chapters 5-7) shows a potential for A15 to be on the critical path. Suppose that the probability that A15 will be critical is .30 (30 percent) with Medium Crane. That is, there is a .70 chance that A15 will not be critical. Further, assume the project model shows that with the greater capacity of the larger crane, A15 has only a .20 probability of becoming critical and a delaying the project. Table 2.1 represents best judgments about delay times versus crane size in the event the path containing A15 becomes critical.

Payoff Table

The Medium Crane rents for $10,000, and the Large Crane for $15,000. For simplicity we will ignore any crew cost savings with the more efficient larger crane. Each day's delay in project completion costs $5,000.

Expected value delay time is calculated by multiplying delay days by the probability of each, then summing. If the decision is made to use the Medium Crane, the probability of no delay is .70; the probability of long delay is (1 - .70) x .20 = .06, and so forth.

The cost incurred if there is a delay is the delay length times the daily delay penalty. For example, a long delay with the Medium Crane costs 10 days x $5,000 per day = $50,000.

Which crane size should the project manager choose?

Table 2.2 — Payoff Table for Crane Size Selection.

Delay Outcome	Medium Crane			Large Crane		
	Proba-bility	Delay Cost	Pr x Cost	Proba-bility	Delay Cost	Pr x Cost
No Delay	.70	0	0	.80	0	0
Long Delay	.06	$50,000	$3,000	.04	$15,000	$600
Medium Delay	.15	25,000	3,750	.10	10,000	1,000
Short Delay	.09	10,000	900	.06	5,000	300
Expected Value Delay Cost			7,650			1,900
Crane Cost			10,000			15,000
Total Expected Value Crane Cost			17,650			16,900

Table 2.2 shows a payoff table evaluation. This is a convenient way to portray simple problems. In this example, only costs apply, so the EMV decision rule translates to:

Choose the alternative having the lowest expected value cost.

EV's are calculated by multiplying cost outcomes times the respective probabilities of occurrence, then summing. EV delay costs are $7,650 for the Medium Crane and $1,900 the Large Crane. These are added to the crane rental costs to arrive at total EV crane costs of $17,650 and $16,900, respectively. The Large Crane is the preferred solution, as its EV cost is $750 less than the Medium Crane.

Decision Tree

Decision tree analysis is a standard calculation tool in decision analysis. Decision trees can accommodate more complex problems than can payoff tables. The diagram graphically represents and assists in calculating expected values.

Decision points are drawn as squares, and chance events are drawn as circles. Figure 2.3 shows a decision tree analysis for the crane size problem. Decision trees are flexible in expressing the logic of a complex decision. Decision tree analysis will be featured in Chapters 3 and 4.

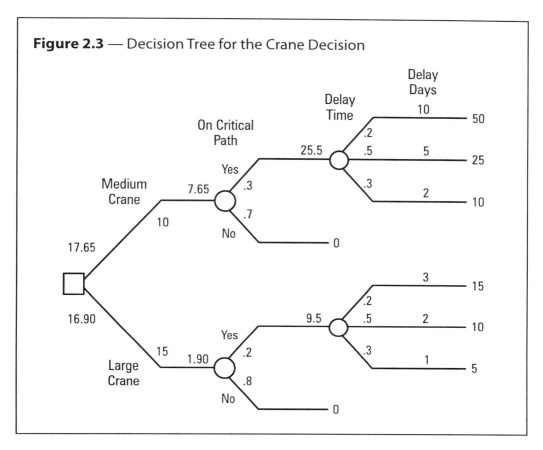

Figure 2.3 — Decision Tree for the Crane Decision

For most people, combining values and probabilities is difficult with unaided intuition. The crane size decision shows the power of simple decision analysis where intuition and conventional analysis fall short.

Summary

Two decision models have been presented, a payoff table and a decision tree. The payoff table works adequately in simple decision models involving a single decision point, several alternatives, and several discrete outcomes. Usually, the chance events in these tables apply symmetrically to every alternative.

Decision trees are better able to represent sequences of chance events and subsequent decision points. A problem's structure is often different for each alternative, and this presents no problem with trees.

There are other evaluation tools, notably Monte Carlo simulation, that can accommodate continuous probability distributions and more sophisticated decision rules.

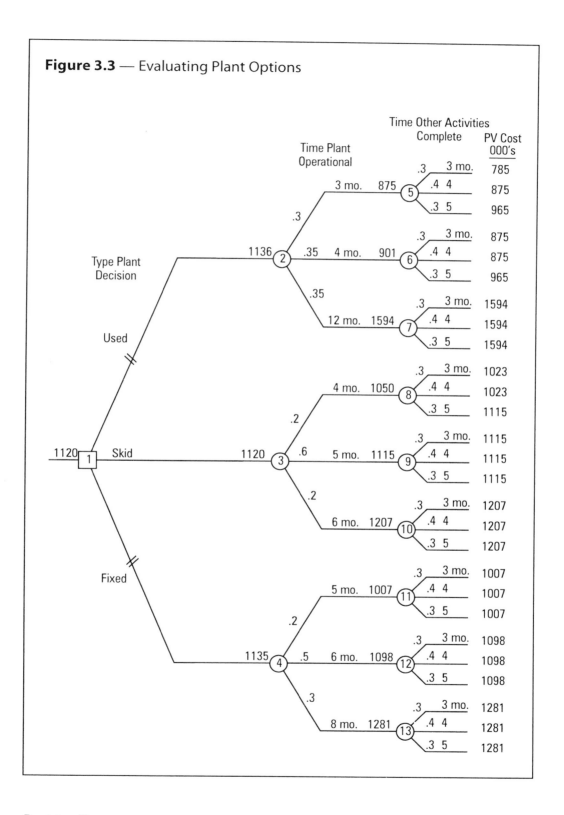

Figure 3.3 — Evaluating Plant Options

Table 3.4. Back-Solving the Tree

EV(5)	=	.3(785)	+	.4(875)	+	.3(965)	= $875,000
EV(6)	=	.3(875)	+	.4(875)	+	.3(965)	= 901,000
EV(7)	=	.3(1594)	+	.4(1594)	+	.3(1594)	= 1,594,000
EV(8)	=	.3(1023)	+	.4(1023)	+	.3(1115)	= 1,050,000
EV(9)	=	.3(1115)	+	.4(1115)	+	.3(1115)	= 1,115,000
EV(10)	=	.3(1207)	+	.4(1207)	+	.3(1207)	= 1,207,000
EV(11)	=	.3(1007)	+	.4(1007)	+	.3(1007)	= 1,007,000
EV(12)	=	.3(1098)	+	.4(1098)	+	.3(1098)	= 1,098,000
EV(13)	=	.3(1281)	+	.4(1281)	+	.3(1281)	= 1,281,000
EV(2)	=	.3 EV(5)	+	.35 EV(6)	+	.35 EV(7)	
	=	.3(875)	+	.35(901)	+	.35(1594)	= $1,136,000
EV(3)	=	.2 EV(8)	+	.6 EV(9)	+	.2 EV(10)	
	=	.2(1050)	+	.6(1115)	+	.2(1207)	= $1,120,000
EV(4)	=	.2 EV(11)	+	.5 EV(12)	+	.3 EV(13)	
	=	.2(1007)	+	.5(1098)	+	.3(1281)	= $1,135,000

And applying the EV decision rule:
EV(1) = Minimum{EV(2), EV(3), EV(4)}
     = Minimum{1136, 1120, 1135} = $1,120,000

Values are shown to the nearest $1,000, although calculations were performed with greater precision.

The model underlying the values shown in Figure 3.3 include, in addition to the assumptions in Tables 3.1-3.3, such items as inflation, cost of capital, depreciation, and taxes.

Try Your Intuition

If you have experience in problems of this sort, perhaps you can judge the best alternative by inspection. Try estimating EV costs for each option. What is the difference in EV cost between the first choice and the next best alternative?

For most of us, even this small problem is much too complex to internalize in our heads. The plant choice is not obvious because each alternative has advantages:

Used Lowest initial cost.

Skid Fastest and lowest-risk acquisition time, medium operating costs, highest salvage value.

Fixed Lowest operating costs, medium investment.

No single alternative dominates across all attributes. Most of us need an analytic tool to have confidence in our selection.

Evaluating Options

The *appraisal approach* of decision analysis is a logical way to evaluate the three plant acquisition alternatives. Figure 3.3 shows the complete decision tree model: terminal nodes (right column) show outcomes if the respective tree path is realized; the outcome value is PV costs. Again, these terminal values are obtained from a cash flow projection model. Since all monetary values are costs, one may work with EV costs instead of EMV's; minimizing EV cost is exactly equivalent to maximizing EMV.

The root node is the Type Plant decision. There are two chance events affecting outcome value: Time Plant Becomes Operational *and* Time Other Activities Complete. The latest event controls when the mine development project is complete. These chance event outcomes are annotated with labels (months to complete) and the probability of the respective outcome. Each chance and decision node is annotated with its EV cost.

The three alternatives are evaluated by back-solving the decision tree. The nodes have been numbered for illustrating the calculations. Table 3.4 shows the sequence and components of node EV calculations.

Note there are fewer calculations at each column of nodes in progressing from right to left through the tree. For large trees, the progressive thinning of branches provides considerable **calculation efficiency** (as compared to a payoff table approach). Acquiring a Skid plant ($1,120,000) appears the best of the three alternatives, although its superiority is slight ($16,000). The "cut" marks on branches indicate inferior alternatives that have been "pruned."

Summary

Decision tree analysis is a convenient way to analyze project decisions having one or several important uncertainties. Probability distributions are used to encode judgments about risk and uncertainty. For all but the simplest of problems, such decision models greatly bolster our intuition.

A single value measure, gauging benefits or progress toward the organization's objective, is a central idea in decision analysis. Money is a convenient measurement scale for most purposes. The Wastewater Plant example combined cost, schedule and performance criteria into a single monetary value measure, EV costs:

- *Schedule* was translated into cost-equivalents by recognizing the value lost due to project delay.
- *Performance* was recognized by different plant operating costs during the mine life.

Many practitioners believe that insights gained into decision problems are more important than the numerical results. Further comfort comes from credible quantitative analysis results.

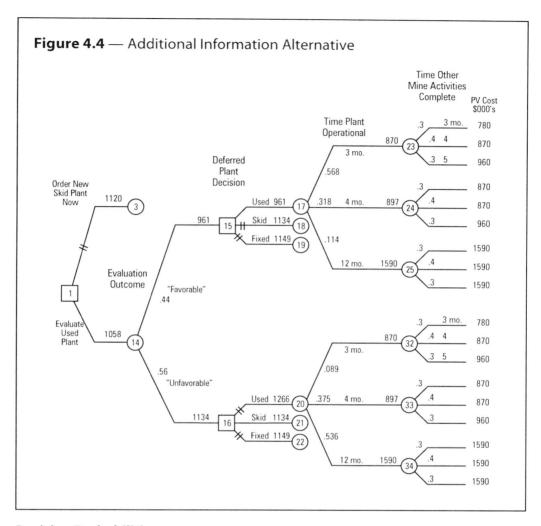

Figure 4.4 — Additional Information Alternative

Revising Probabilities

The used plant evaluation and testing provide information useful for revising the prior probability assessments in the Time Plant Operational nodes. Note the evaluation node in this section of the tree is followed by the investment decision to show whether new information adds value. If the alternative to implement is already known, further information and analysis is pointless. Additional information adds value to the project *only* if it has the *potential to change what you are going to do.*

For simplicity, the evaluation results are classified into two outcomes: "Favorable" and "Unfavorable." Project engineers judge the [2] *quality* of this imperfect information as shown in Figure 4.3. These nodes are not numbered; this tree is a side calculation intermediate step. The sequence of these two nodes will be reversed in the decision model. The probabilities for the evaluation outcomes

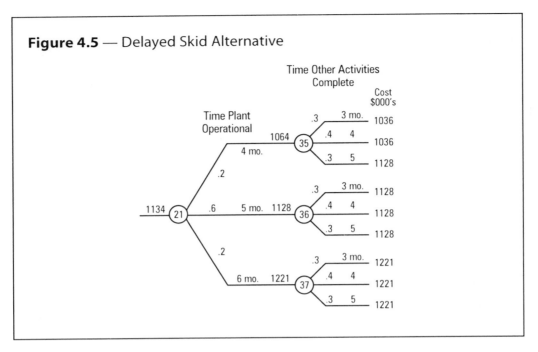

Figure 4.5 — Delayed Skid Alternative

are assessed *conditioned* upon the Time Plant Operational event outcomes. Representing conditional probabilities is a convenient and powerful feature of decision trees.

The order of nodes in Figure 4.3 is the logical way to express the assessments and relationships between the two events. The sequence is in reverse order from what is needed to solve our real world problem. The actual sequence would be:

- Get the evaluation result
- Make the plant decision
- Experience how long it takes to complete the plant.

We need to reverse or *invert the nodes* from the sequence in which the probabilities are assessed. This is done with a straightforward technique called **Bayesian revision** (using Bayes' theorem; see sidebar, Bayesian Process). We revise the prior probabilities about Time Plant Operational based upon the Evaluation Outcome. The original and revised probabilities for each Time Plant Operational outcome are shown in Table 4.1 and in Figure 4.4.

Evaluating the New Alternative

Figure 4.4 shows the decision model extended for the Evaluate Used Plant alternative. The values on the right of the diagram are terminal values: present value costs for the respective paths through the tree and include any penalty for value lost for a delayed mine opening.

Figure 4.5 details the calculations for the expected value cost of the delayed Skid alternative given the Examine Used Plant choice. This value changed from $1.120 million to $1.134 million because of

Bayesian Process

For readers interested in how prior probability assessments are revised based upon new information, here is a brief explanation. The process is credited to Rev. Thomas Bayes, an 18th century British clergyman. Bayes' theorem is most often

$$P(e_i \mid A) = \frac{P(A \mid e_i) P(e_i)}{\sum_{j=1}^{N} P(A \mid e_j) P(e_j)}$$

where,

e_i = outcome of the chance event of interest

A = attribute (additional information) and,

$P(A \mid e_i)$ is read as "the probability of A given ei."

While the formula is more ominous than difficult, a more convenient solution technique is to construct and inspect a **joint probability** table. The two nodes in Figure 4.3 can be expressed in the following table.

Joint Probability Table

		Evaluation Outcome		
		"Favorable"	"Unfavorable"	
Months to Complete Plant	3	.25	.05	.30
	4	.14	.21	.35
	12	.05	.30	.35
		.44	.56	1.00

The values inside the table are the joint probabilities, i.e., probabilities for the compound events comprised of combinations of Evaluation Outcome and Months to Complete Plant as shown in Figure 4.3.

The probabilities for the inverted tree, can be read from the table. Assume, for example, we have a "Favorable" Evaluation Outcome. There is a .44 chance of this occurring. When it does, we are restricted to the left column of the table, which has three possibilities for Months to Complete Plant: 3, 4, or 12. The probabilities of the Months to Complete Plant outcomes are in proportion to .25, .14, and .05. These values, however, do not sum to 1; each must be *normalized* to total 1. This is accomplished by dividing each number by the column total. The normalized numbers represent the *revised probabilities* conditioned on the "Favorable" Evaluation Outcome.

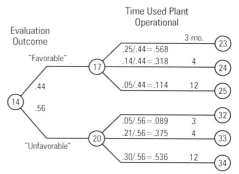

Inverted Probability Tree

For clarity, the information event outcomes are in quotes.

the added evaluation cost (about $18,000 after-tax) less the present value timing adjustment (about $4,000) of delayed investment.

New information adds value only if it has the potential to change a decision. In this example, the project manager should choose to install the Used Plant, instead of the Skid Plant, if the evaluation result is "Favorable."

The Evaluate Used Plant option is the best alternative. Spending $30,000 pre-tax on inspection adds a net $62,000 ($1.120-$1.058 million) of after-tax value to the project.

The decision tree was back-solved to compute the expected value cost for each alternative. Starting at the right, each chance node is replaced (and annotated) with its EV cost. Each decision node is presumed replaced with its best alternative. Here are several example calculations, starting at the upper-right of Figure 4.4 and working backward:

$$EV(23) = \$870,000 = .3(780) + .4(870) + .3(960)$$
$$EV(17) = \$961,000 = .568(870) + .318(897) + .114(1590)$$
$$EV(15) = \$961,000 = \text{minimum of } (961,1134,1149)$$
$$EV(14) = \$1,058,000 = .44(961) + .56(1134)$$

Summary

Many projects have a sequence of decision points. Analyzing these options is an extremely important part of an evaluation. Decision trees are especially useful for analyzing situations with decision points after additional information will become known.

The wastewater plant decision tree analysis was extended to value an alternative to get more information. Many projects have opportunities to improve value through such additional data gathering and analysis. In most cases, it is convenient to structure the decision model using the new information to revise prior probabilities. Alternatively, one can revise assessments for event outcome values. This usually involves modeling the system to understand and quantify the relationship between the information event (symptom) and the chance event of interest. Occasionally it is appropriate to revise *both* event probabilities and values.

Fairly complex problems can be handled in an orderly way with decision tree analysis. For some problems, the tree can become exceedingly large. The preeminent calculation alternative for such cases is Monte Carlo simulation.

Table 5.3 — Input Distributions

Input Variable	Discrete Distributions (Decision Trees)	Continuous* Distributions (Monte Carlo Simulation)	Units
Time to Complete Other Activities	{.3, 3; .4, 4; .3, 5}	Normal (4, .775)	Months
Time to Complete Skid Unit	{.2, 4; .6, 5; .2, 6}	Normal (5, .632)	Months
Time to Complete Fixed Unit	{.2, 5; .5, 6; .3, 8}	3.067+(10) Beta (2, 4)	Months
Time to Complete Used Unit	{.3, 3; .35, 4; .35, 12}	1+(27.5) Beta (2, 8)	Months
Used Unit Estimation Error		Normal (1, .3)	Estimate Factor
Delay Cost		Normal (150, 22.5)	$000/Month

* The normal distribution is specified by mean, standard deviation. The base beta distributions range from 0–1 and have shapes determined by α_1, and α_2 shape factors: $x^{1-\alpha_1} (1-x)^{1-\alpha_2}$

Table 5.4 Expected Value Costs

Alternative	$000's EV Costs
Fixed Now	1130
Skid Now	1120
Used Now	1141
Fixed Later	1143
Skid Later	1136
Used Later	1137
Evaluate Used	1024

Simulation allows a rich representation of risks and uncertainties. Virtually any number of chance events can be incorporated into the model. This is unlike decision trees, which can quickly become too large to solve.

To further embellish the wastewater plant example, another chance event, Delay Cost, was added. This is the per-month financial impact of delayed (or accelerated) project mine startup.

Table 5.3 shows the various distributions used in the simulation model. Note the discrete distributions used before are now represented by either *normal* or *beta* distributions with specific values for

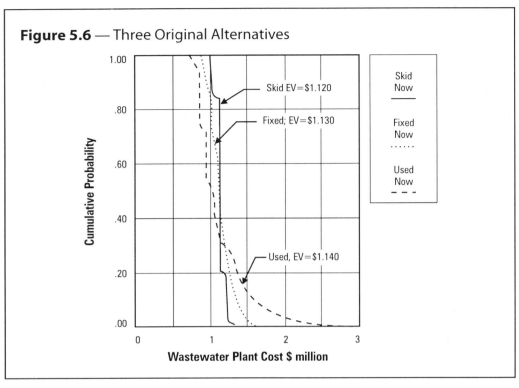

Figure 5.6 — Three Original Alternatives

Cumulative Probability (y-axis)

Skid EV=$1.120
Fixed; EV=$1.130
Used, EV=$1.140

Wastewater Plant Cost $ million (x-axis)

Skid Now

Fixed Now

Used Now

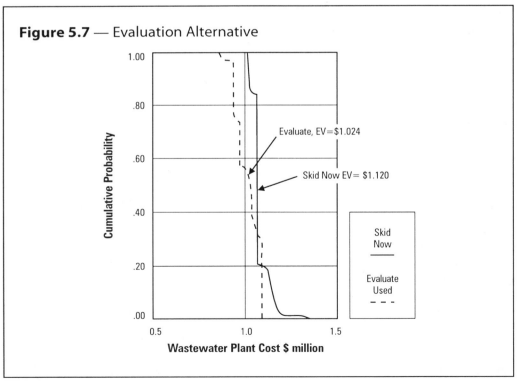

Figure 5.7 — Evaluation Alternative

Cumulative Probability (y-axis)

Evaluate, EV=$1.024
Skid Now EV= $1.120

Wastewater Plant Cost $ million (x-axis)

Skid Now

Evaluate Used

each parameter involved. The normal distribution has two parameters (mean, standard deviation). Beta distributions are simple functions that can be tailored (with two shape exponents) to resemble many shapes ranging from a symmetric, normal-distribution-looking distribution to highly skewed (asymmetric) distributions. Here, beta distributions provide asymmetric bell-shaped distributions with *positive skewness* (longest tail on the positive side).

Results

Table 5.4 shows the results of a 500-trial simulation run. The numbers, while close to those obtained from the decision tree analysis, are somewhat different due to the increased detail of the continuous distributions and the added Delay Cost variable. The Used Later cost is lower than the Used Now cost because, in this model, the testing and inspecting cost ($30,000, including deposit) is expensed rather than capitalized for taxes. This cost, however, reduces the investment required if this alternative is chosen after inspection.

Without the Evaluate Used option, the decision would be made today by comparing the distributions for the three base plant alternatives. Figure 5.6 shows the cumulative probability curves [2] for these options. The Skid alternative has a slight advantage in having the lowest expected value cost. The skid plant also is the least risky (risk evidenced by the width of the distribution). The *stair steps* are caused by the monthly time periods in the cash flow projection model.

It is also an option to inspect the used plant before committing to a choice. After taking one month to do this evaluation, the remaining alternatives would be compared. Fixed and Skid alternatives would be delayed one month, slightly increasing their expected value costs. The Used alternative is also reassessed, based upon the evaluation information. The decision policy would be to choose the alternative having the lowest expected value cost. Figure 5.7 compares the Evaluate Used alternative with the Skid alternative. Pursuing the information alternative, Evaluate Used, adds $96,000 of value to the project [3].

Simulation in Practice

Simulation is excellent for determining the distribution curves for various outcome parameters of interest. Figure 5.8 shows a histogram of simulation results for the improvement offered by the evaluate alternative. Superimposed on the figure is the cumulative distribution. Random sampling and the accumulation buckets typically result in an irregular distribution shape. Although the histogram appears lumpy, this has little impact on the EV calculation [4]. The cumulative curve appears smoother because it avoids the time bucket effect and dilutes any random sampling errors. Cumulative curves are used, in general, to compare the risk-versus-value profiles of the different alternatives. The simulation model used for this analysis uses discrete, monthly time periods. This contributed to the discontinuities in the resulting distributions. Without too much effort, the

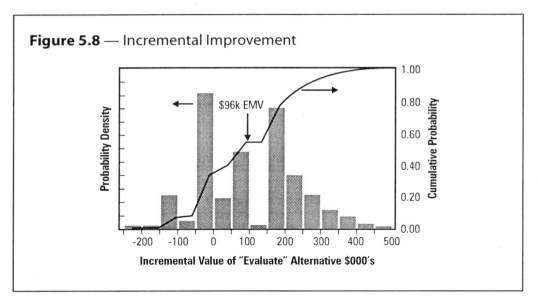

Figure 5.8 — Incremental Improvement

Probability Density

$96k EMV

Cumulative Probability

1.00
0.80
0.60
0.40
0.20
0.00

-200 -100 0 100 200 300 400 500

Incremental Value of "Evaluate" Alternative $000's

model could be modified to use weeks, days, hours, etc., to meet the precision requirements of the study.

To minimize computer running time while increasing detail, there are sampling techniques generally described as "design of experiments" (see Chapter 6). A closely allied technique called Latin Hypercube Sampling (LHS) has become very popular in recent years. This is a hybrid between *uniform sampling* and traditional *Monte Carlo sampling*. LHS typically reduces the number of simulation trials to obtain a desired answer precision by a factor of about three.

Summary

Monte Carlo simulation is a complementary calculation alternative to decision tree analysis. Each technique has its advantages and disadvantages. The nature of the problem at hand, available tools, and personal preference determine the choice of method. *Simulation is usually preferred* in situations:

- Having many significant uncertainties and contingencies
- Involving a portfolio (e.g., strategic decisions involving a collection of projects)
- Where outcome probability distributions are desired, providing additional insights and for comparing risk-versus-value profiles
- Involving multiple decision criteria in situations where it is difficult or undesirable to condense several criteria to a single value (objective) function. (Chapter 10 explores multi-criteria decisions.)

In contrast, *decision trees are usually preferred* for situations:

- Involving a sequence of decisions (e.g., value of information problems)

- Where correlations between chance events will be represented by Bayesian calculations (i.e., revising prior probabilities based upon new information using Bayes' theorem)
- Where a simple decision model will suffice (often, decision analysts start with a decision tree model and then move to simulation when the model becomes more complex).

Simulation and decision trees are the principal decision analysis computation techniques. Each solves for expected values, but do so in very different ways.

Chapter Six

Other Probabilistic Techniques

Decision tree analysis and Monte Carlo simulation are the most popular calculation techniques for evaluations under uncertainty. There are other quantitative techniques useful in dealing with uncertainty in specific situations. One method employs what might be called pseudo-probability distributions. Others provide alternate ways of working with probability distributions.

Summary of Methods

Table 6.1 lists decision analysis and related techniques, along with their key strengths and weaknesses. This chapter profiles these methods:
- Dynamic project modeling with Monte Carlo simulation
- Parameter method and moments method
- Fuzzy logic
- Approximate integration.

The last two of these methods are emerging technologies and are likely to become important in project management. The methods listed in the lower part of Table 6.1 are useful at times, but for our purposes will be only briefly mentioned.

Critical Path Method (**CPM**) [1] and Program Evaluation and Review Technique (**PERT**) [2] are the classic modeling techniques for controlling project schedule. Both identify the deterministic critical path. PERT is CPM with the substitution of probability distributions for activity completion times. In both cases, slack times are calculated for activities that lie off the deterministic critical path. The principal drawbacks of PERT are:
- It does not recognize that activities outside the deterministic critical path can be late and delay the project;
- Real-world projects are often inadequately represented by a simple network of independent [3] activities.

Table 6.1 — Techniques of Uncertainty

METHOD	KEY STRENGTHS	KEY WEAKNESSES
Discussed in Previous Chapters		
Decision Tree Analysis	Graphical calculation. of expected value	Must convert continuous into discrete distributions
	Evaluating alternatives with sequential decisions (e.g., value of information)	Must limit number of chance event outcomes
		Requires value function
Monte Carlo Simulation	Can accommodate complexity easily, such as dynamic behavior under contingencies	Time vs. accuracy trade-off. Solution can be computationally time-consuming
	Very generally applicable	Solution is approximate and sometimes difficult to duplicate
Discussed in This Chapter		
Parameter Method; Method of Moments	Medium complexity Fast reproducible solutions	Provides only statistics about the shape of the solution distribution
		Difficult to deal with subsequent decision points, correlations and non-linearities
Monte Carlo Simulation	(see MCS above in table)	(see MCS above in table)
Fuzzy Logic	Low-medium complexity Fast	Only approximates probabilistic reasoning
	Reproducible solutions	Potential developments needed to improve accuracy
Approximate Integration	Fast Repeatable solution	Little recognition in practice and literature. Emerging technique
Identified in This Chapter		
CPM, PERT, and PDM	Simple	Simplistic project network model may be inadequate
		Only one critical path is recognized
Scenario Analysis	Simple	Seldom quantifies risks and uncertainties
Sensitivity Analysis	Simple	Does not recognize risk vs. value trade-offs
Design of Experiments	Value optimizing or variance reduction with efficient handling of many decision (controllable) variables	Limited representation of Taguchi uncertainty, "noise," e.g., using "Low" and "High" for each chance event
Multi-Criteria Approaches; Analytic Hierarchy Process	Simple if non-probabilistic	Risk or uncertainty is merely one of several attributes; problems with consistency.
		Probabilities can be used if a *value function* is devised.
Influence Diagram	Similar to decision trees	More difficult theory and calculations
	Better expresses relationships between variables	

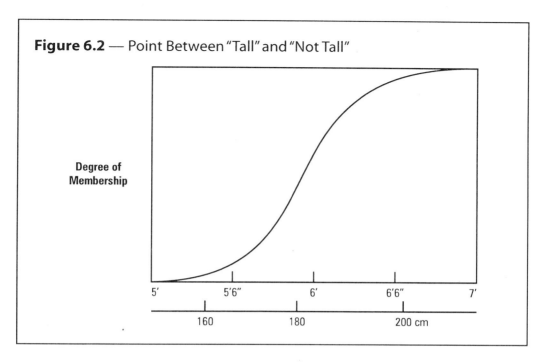

Figure 6.2 — Point Between "Tall" and "Not Tall"

Degree of
Membership

5'   5'6"   6'   6'6"   7'

160   180   200 cm

formation. Membership measures the confidence that the proposition "tall" is true. While the membership function is not equivalent to a probability distribution, they appear similar in ways.

A **confidence factor** is a number, ranging from 0 to 1, representing the degree of confidence in an input assessment. Similarly, confidence factors (CF's) can be assigned to assertions, rules and the resultant *inferences*. The 0-1 range, which has the same bounds of a probability, *does not* have the same meaning as probability. A 1 CF means 100 percent probability. However, CF=0 means only that the information has no value; it does not mean that the opposite outcome (complement) must be true. Confidence factors have been widely used in *expert systems* to encode the reliability of assertions, rules, and inferences. (An expert system is a computer program that contains expert knowledge about a narrow problem which allows a non-expert operator to perform a particular task at a proficiency similar to a human expert [10].)

Instead of crisp, single-value inputs, project projections can include assumptions expressed as fuzzy propositions. Fuzzy set calculations propagate quickly through a model. The result is membership functions for value, cost, schedule, etc. Figure 6.3 shows the outcome result of a simple project model. The fuzzy results propagate through the model in all calculations. The solution is fast and reproducible.

The main drawback is that the *calculations do not have the logical rigor of probability theory*. One obtains strange "distribution" shapes from seemingly innocent combinations of variables. Nearly unpredictable results occur with complex formulas and conditional branching (*IF* statements).

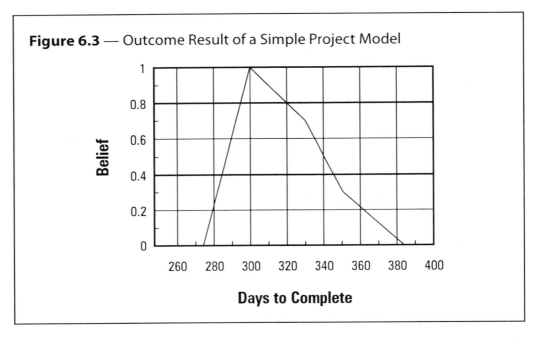

Figure 6.3 — Outcome Result of a Simple Project Model

Fuzzy logic's mathematical operations are somewhat arbitrary and may be improved eventually. Expect further applications of fuzzy logic for making projections as the techniques become better understood and refined [11].

Approximate Integration

Although the technique is very general, Monte Carlo simulation gives only an approximate solution. The result is sometimes slow to converge with additional trials. Further, regenerating an earlier solution is often impractical, thus making it more difficult to value incremental improvements.

Ideally, the EV integral could be assaulted directly with symbolic mathematics. This would provide exact solutions to project models. However, this is impossible with most decision problems.

Numeric integration holds promise. The results are reproducible and fast. The method is known by several names: *convolution, quadrature*, or *cubic spline integration* (splines were flexible strips of wood used by draftsmen). Another term is *fast calculus integration*.

Approximate integration provides suitably accurate results for simple probabilistic models involving addition and multiplication. One obtains the solution directly, in the form of an outcome probability distribution. The signal processing field has used these calculation techniques for 25 years, and they are now emerging as possible methods for decision analysis.

Other Probabilistic Techniques

Chapter Seven

Modeling Techniques
(Part I)

*Decision analysis and the associated techniques help deci-
sion makers choose wisely under conditions of uncertainty.*

Decision analysis is applicable when:
- *The situation has two or more alternatives.*
- *At least one alternative has multiple possible outcomes.*
- *The range of possible outcomes is significant enough to
warrant attention to the decision.*

*This chapter focuses upon quantifying the outcome values.
Most often, a model is constructed and used to project different
possible futures. Each projection, or scenario, is summarized
into an outcome value. This single value measures goodness
or progress toward the organization's objective [1].*

Forecasts From Models

It can be said that forecasting the future is the most important analytic problem in business. Nearly every decision presupposes a forecast of what will happen with each alternative.

A *projection* is a scenario that reflects a set of assumptions. A
model predicts what will happen if the assumption values are realized. These assumptions may be forecasts of the input variables or
merely what-if values. A *forecast* is a projection based upon forecasts
of the individual input assumptions. And although forecast and prediction are synonymous, forecast is preferred because it implies an
analytic process of estimation and calculation. In the context of this
discussion of decision analysis, the best *forecast* is the EV outcome.

In addition to input values, the forecast includes assumptions
about *structure* of the system. This structure is captured in the fabric
of the project model, for example, the work breakdown structure.

Forecasting Approaches

There are three general approaches to forecasting:
- Intuition or guessing
- Extrapolating the past, such as by linear regression
- Modeling the system, and then using the model to generate a forecast.

Intuition provides forecasts of questionable value. The prediction is believable only if the source person has recognized superior experience and a record of reasonably accurate judgments. Seldom are the assumptions or reasoning adequately stated. Because intuition is hard to define, it is difficult to achieve consensus and to train successors.

Extrapolation requires suitable historical data and is based on the *ceteris paribus* (all other things being the same) assumption. This implies that conditions tomorrow will be like conditions yesterday.

Modeling involves designing and building a representation of the system. The model is an abstraction of the real world based upon one's best understanding. Modeling is particularly valuable in situations that are new, unique or complex.

Most often, forecast are based upon some set of initial assumptions. Examples include activity costs and completion times. Single-value input assumptions result in a single-value outcome when calculated through the project model. Recall that such models are termed *deterministic* because every value is *singly determined*.

Deterministic Cash Flow Model

This chapter outlines decision making from the perspective of a business enterprise, although the techniques apply to all entity types.

In business, value derives from cash flow. The present value (PV) calculation transforms an incremental cash flow forecast into incremental corporate value. Presumably, this cash flow is available to distribute to investors or to reinvest in the business. Discounted cash flow (DCF) analysis is the basis for most modern financial analysis, although there are many arguable details, such as inflation, tax, and cost of capital assumptions. The general process, however, is straightforward.

Chapter 2 examined how decision policy is a statement about how to value outcomes. Project managers are traditionally concerned with performance, schedule, and cost. One needs a logical way to trade-off one dimension in terms of another. While these dimensions are important, it is impossible to make consistent decisions without a way to determine a composite value.

A single value measure is needed. The recommended approach, for most purposes, is converting non-monetary dimensions into money equivalents. This is the simplest way to deal with multiple objectives or multiple decision criteria. Thus, project performance and schedule translate into cash flow impact and are combined with costs. This single value measure approach is illustrated in Figure 7.1.

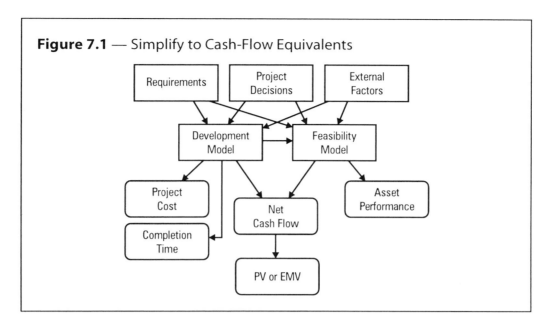

Figure 7.1 — Simplify to Cash-Flow Equivalents

Shaded blocks indicate commonly generated outcomes that inherently lead to multi-criteria decision making. Information generated in the development model and feasibility model can be used to generate net cash flow and, ultimately, the PV or EMV.

Problem and Model Scope

A good project model contains sufficient operating and financial detail as to reasonably represent the impacts of the relevant decision alternatives. The appropriate level of detail depends upon the decision at hand. Sometimes a quick inspection of the model outputs will indicate an obvious decision. In other situations, the relative differences in outcome values may be small. When this is the case, further analysis effort is warranted, perhaps incorporating further detail in the model.

The model's *scope* is one of the most important analysis design decisions. The system being analyzed may be all or part of an industry, business, project or transaction. The scope usually needs to consider the remaining life-cycle of the project and sometimes the life-cycle of the product of the project as illustrated in Figure 7.2. Decision analysis techniques are fully general, and apply to construction or non-construction projects equally. Sometimes managers concern themselves only with a development or construction phase, which is usually inadequate. Completion time and asset performance also impact value by affecting cash flows. Decision analysis techniques are fully general, and apply to construction or non-construction projects equally. All important details and aspects of the problem should be incorporated into the model, at least to the point where the best alternative is clear.

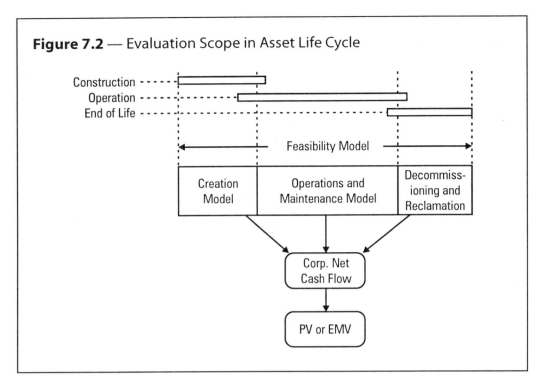

Figure 7.2 — Evaluation Scope in Asset Life Cycle

Projects often impact other areas of corporate operations and even other projects. Simplifying assumptions are almost always necessary. We want to avoid modeling the entire corporation for every decision. However, sufficient detail is needed to adequately forecast the impact on corporate net cash flow. Incremental cash flow effect is generally the most useful model outcome. Accuracy is usually better regarding the *difference* between alternatives than for the actual alternative values.

The Modeling Process

Initially, a problem is identified. Often, a decision arises because something happens or because a new idea or information surfaces. It usually involves a choice about allocating resources such as time, money, or materials. The situation may be that a modest effort or investment potentially frees or safeguards much greater resources.

Increasingly, the value of *proactively creating new alternatives* is being recognized. Professionals should continually ask, "What can we do to improve the value of this project?" And, "What might happen different from plan, and what can we do to protect from or exploit the contingency?"

Often, a cross-discipline project team is involved or assigned to the problem. The team should first define the problem and include a situation description. The scope of the problem-solving process is important. The need to estimate incremental corporate value drives the scope of the decision model.

Chapter Nine

Judgments and Biases

*Psychology is often a part of decision science: many investigators are interested in better understanding how people **do** make decisions. We would like to avoid biases and cognitive illusions. Our efforts here are to teach how people **should** make decisions.*

Decision analysis is a quantitative discipline. Previous chapters describe forecast and evaluation models. This chapter focuses on the expert judgments that are inputs to these models.

Three Roles

There are three roles in the decision process, as shown in Figure 9.1:
- *Experts* or *assessors* provide the judgments that go into an evaluation. Usually, the most knowledgeable people available provide these inputs.
- *Evaluation analysts* are primarily responsible for developing the quantitative project models, models that generate scenario outcomes and forecasts for each alternative.
- *Decision makers* review the forecasts and judge whether the analysis is credible. They make the selection (usually accepting the team's recommendation) and initiate implementation.
  Overlapping roles are common.

Judgments

A *judgment* is a value assessment performed by a person. There are two basic approaches to judgments, or assessments, as inputs to an evaluation:
- Non-probabilistic (deterministic) [1]
  — Single point values (e.g., a particular cost)
  — Single line forecasts (e.g., inflation rate over time).
    A conventional deterministic analysis uses only best input variable forecasts. Even in decision analysis, this is adequate to

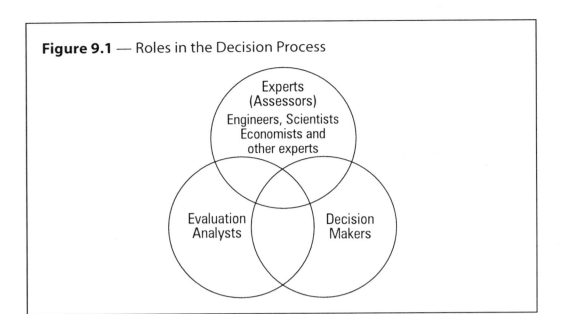

Figure 9.1 — Roles in the Decision Process

Experts
(Assessors)
Engineers, Scientists
Economists and
other experts

Evaluation
Analysts

Decision
Makers

represent minor variables or those with known with high confidence.

- Probabilistic (stochastic)
  — Continuous probability distributions (e.g., hours to complete an activity)
  — Discrete probability distributions (e.g., number of subcontractors bidding)
  — Event probabilities, that is, whether the event happens or not (e.g., whether a task will require rework).

When a value is uncertain, the representation takes the form of a probability distribution. Considering a single variable, alone, a probability distribution can represent an expert's entire judgment about the possible outcomes of a chance event.

Risk analysis is often used to mean the process of assessing the probability distribution for a *single* variable.

Objective and Subjective Probability

Because a judgment is performed by a human, the resulting probability distribution is called a *subjective probability*.

The extreme opposite is *objective probability*. This is supported by a comprehensive understanding of the system or conclusive evidence: either knowing the value and likelihood of every possible element in the population, or completely understanding the stochastic process providing variable outcome values.

The continuum between the two extremes is shown in Figure 9.2. Most judgments lie somewhere in the middle, far from either end. Even with considerable data from similar situations, the expert must assess to what degree the data still apply.

- **Insensitivity to sample size**. Often there is insufficient data to draw a conclusion. People are prone to hasty generalization.
- **Availability bias**. We remember cases that are more famous or where we were more closely involved. Some scenarios are easier to imagine than others, such as those in our industry or area of expertise. The most recent data or experience is weighted most heavily. The easier it is to imagine or remember, the higher the believed likelihood of occurrence.
- **Insensitivity to prior probabilities**. Discrepant and unusual events are given undue weight even though rare. Exceptions are remembered and weighted as if commonplace. Judgment bias occurs when the current situation is rare, neither common nor unique.
- **Sensitivity to the cause of the problem**. People are willing to do more to save a species endangered by hunting than endangered by natural change. Life-threatening risks are more acceptable if the person has a choice about being exposed to the risk (e.g., drives a motorcycle without a helmet).
- **Anchoring**. People do not like to change their minds, especially if their earlier position was stated publicly. They "anchor" to the previous position. Later, they are more likely to recognize information that reinforces the original judgment or decision.

  Psychologists have demonstrated that people assessing a probability distribution shape should not try to build around an initial "best guess." The expert inadvertently anchors to the original number. This effect is minimized if the assessment starts at the extremes of the distribution and works inward.
- **Framing**. We are sensitive to the wording and context of outcomes. This is called the *framing* of an event description. Very different judgments can result from the way questions are asked.

  Consider a major project that will earn a $20 million profit for the company if it succeeds, but will lose $2 million dollars if it fails. Asking, "What minimum *probability of success* would you require to be willing to approve this project?" evokes a response different than the complement question, "What maximum *probability of failure* would you accept and still be willing to approve this project?" The responses should add but often do not. Surveys show that people are more adverse to outcomes posed in terms of *losing* jobs or lives when compared to outcomes posed in terms of *saving* jobs or lives.

Improving Evaluations

Consistent, objective evaluations require good analysis practice. Here are some guidelines:
- A conscientious effort should be made to **best capture the experts' judgments** in assessing input variables. Some of these assessments may be highly subjective. Whether additional investigation is warranted can be evaluated as a *value of information* problem (see Chapter 4).

- Strive to avoid judgment biases in assessing input variables. **Everyone upstream from the decision maker should be as objective as possible.** Otherwise, the analysis is questionable and of little value. Note, if everyone is slightly conservative, the resulting analysis can be overwhelmingly conservative.
- Some situations demand conservative decision making. A conservative attitude is a bias — but is often appropriate. **Apply a consistent risk policy.** This is done, in effect, in the final stage of analysis. Most often, the decision maker simply compares risk versus value (or cost) profiles of the different alternatives and chooses the best one (see Chapter 10).
- Certain errors can be detected by **validation.** Models can be devised to validate outcome data. Conversely, input data can be used to validate models.
- In developing a valid model, it helps to **decompose** the project system into sub-models. Quantify subjective assessments, and model interrelationships between variables. A **suitable stochastic method** (e.g., Monte Carlo simulation) correctly propagates the probability distributions throughout the calculations.
- Recognize that biases do exist. Some of these can be avoided or minimized by **carefully structuring the problem**. Use an appropriate value measure, and separate judgments from preferences. A common error, for example, is to increase the present value discount rate to compensate for risk. It is far better to use probabilities to deal with uncertainty, and use the discount rate only to represent preference for time value of money.
- Perhaps the most powerful way to improve decisions is ***post evaluations*** or post-audits. These are follow-up analyses of decisions after the general results become known. There is a psychological bias toward rationalization, and many people have difficulty reconstructing their thought process after learning the outcome. It is important to preserve the original reasoning by documenting the analysis. Provide **performance feedback** to the individual assessors, and use what is learned to improve the evaluation process.

Summary

As professionals, most of us spend a great portion of our workdays processing or preparing information for others to act upon. This work is either evaluation itself, or preparation for evaluation. Employers and clients are better served by ensuring that evaluations are objective—a hallmark of professionalism.

Chapter Ten

Utility and
Multi-Criteria Decisions

*Most business decisions are based upon monetary value. The **cost/benefit/risk analysis** focuses on the calculation of expected monetary value (EMV). Recall that EMV is expected value present value. Maximizing EMV is a suitable decision policy for most business situations.*

Not all circumstances are appropriate for EMV maximizing including:
- *When possible outcome values are large and the decision maker is conservative.*
- *When money is not an appropriate measure. Or, when it's not the sole measure of value and non-money considerations cannot be converted easily into monetary-equivalents.*

*This chapter shows how **utility theory** provides a logical, consistent way to deal with these situations.*

Conservative Risk Attitude

Logical decision making is based upon appraisal. Alternatives are appraised, or valued, and the best one implemented. In evaluating a particular alternative, the value for each possible outcome is calculated. These outcome values are then weighted with their probabilities of occurrence. The probability-weighted average value is the expected value (EV).

In decision analysis, probabilities are used to represent judgments about uncertainty. All of the analysis inputs should be judged as objectively as possible. Properly done, the analysis results in an unbiased distribution of project value (or cost). Assume that monetary value, PV, is the measure of value. The PV distribution shows the range of possible outcomes and their relative likelihood of occurrence. The *risk-neutral* decision maker needs only to know the EV PV (EMV) for each alternative in order to choose the best one. The EMV decision rule would be the organization's decision policy.

Example of Risk Aversion

What does it mean to be "risk neutral" or "conservative?" Suppose a company is having an expensive component manufactured. It is negotiating a cost-plus fabrication contract with the supplying manufacturer. Discussions have been candid, and all data—especially cost details—are being shared. There is a large contingency that potentially will quadruple the fabrication cost. Thus, manufacturing cost is a major uncertainty. With a cost-plus contract, the buyer bears the risk. Assume that other factors, such as performance and schedule, are fixed.

The possible cost outcomes to the buyer, and the probabilities, under the cost-plus contract are:

> Best Outcome   = $1 million cost, p = .90
> Worst Outcome = $4 million cost, p = .10

Then:

> EV cost = .9($1 million) + .1($4 million) = $1.3 million.

(These amounts may be factored to make the outcomes more closely match the scale of costs typically encountered in your business.)

The deal is near being closed when the supplier offers to change the contract to a fixed-cost contract. They ask, "What fixed price would you be willing to pay, instead?"

The correct answer depends on the buyer's attitude towards risk:

- If the company is ***risk-neutral*** it would be *indifferent* between paying a fixed $1.3 million or accepting the cost-plus contract outcomes and risks.
- If the customer is willing to pay somewhat more than the $1.3 million EV cost, then it is conservative or ***risk-averse***. For example, willingness to pay a *risk premium* is common decision behavior. A conservative buyer might agree to a $1.5 million price.
- If the risky, cost-plus contract is preferred to a fixed $1.3 million price, then the company is ***risk-seeking*** in this situation. This is unusual behavior except when there is entertainment value in gambling or when striving to reach a goal. Everyone pays more than the EMV payoff when playing casino games or buying lottery tickets.

Conservative Behavior

Conservative behavior is widespread — almost universal. Should this be an important part of decision policy?

For small decisions, decision makers can afford to be risk-neutral. When the outcomes become large compared to the reference net worth, then the typical decision maker will make substantial value adjustments for risk attitude.

For large, publicly held corporations and governments, risks are shared by many individuals. For these entities, many practitioners believe the EMV decision rule is appropriate.

For individuals and small, closely-held companies, a conservative risk policy is more suitable. Still, day-to-day decisions will be almost exactly the same as the EMV decision rule. However, large decisions may require conservatism. Utility theory describes how to modify an EMV decision analysis for a conservative risk attitude.

Utility is a measure of value reflecting the preferences of the decision maker based upon beliefs and values. The EV concept still applies for decision-making under uncertainty; outcome value, however, is measured in utility units instead of present value (PV). The decision rule is to choose the alternative having the highest expected utility (EU).

Utility Function

Assume that maximizing monetary value is the objective. The *objective* value measure, then, would be PV using an appropriate marginal cost of capital as the discount rate. In the probabilistic sense, the objective measure is EMV.

Risk aversion is exhibited in what economists call the *law of diminishing marginal utility*. As an example, for most persons, winning a $1 million prize would be a tremendously exciting event. If one already has $10 million, however, the added $1 million would hardly be noticed. Incremental positive amounts add incrementally less value as wealth is accumulated.

For conservative persons, value is *not* a linear function of PV; twice the positive PV does not represent twice as much value. A utility equation or graph is needed to convert PV dollars into another measure of value. Economist and decision theorists use the word *utility* synonymously with *value*. Utility units are often called *utils*.

The curve shown in Figure 10.1 is an example utility function. It translates *objective* value, PV (x-axis), into **perceived value**, utility (y-axis). The y-axis scale is arbitrary, including choice of origin. An upward-sloping straight line represents the utility function of a risk-neutral decision maker where value is proportionate to PV. Utility curves that are concave downward represent conservative risk attitudes.

Many decision analysts scale the y-axis so that the worst possible outcome has utility = 0, and the best possible outcome has utility = 1. The curve, regardless of shape or scale, is usually deduced from the decision maker's answers to a series of hypothetical decision problems.

The author prefers a form of utility equation where value measured in somewhat tangible units: *risk-neutral* **(RN) dollars**. This makes the utility measure more meaningful:

RN$ -1 million cost is 1 million times worse than a $1 cost.

RN$+1 million benefit is 1 million times better than a $1 benefit.

Note that for positive PV's (benefits), incremental utility value decreases as PV's gets larger. Costs or losses are amplified for negative PV's.

Figure 10.1 — Example Utility Function

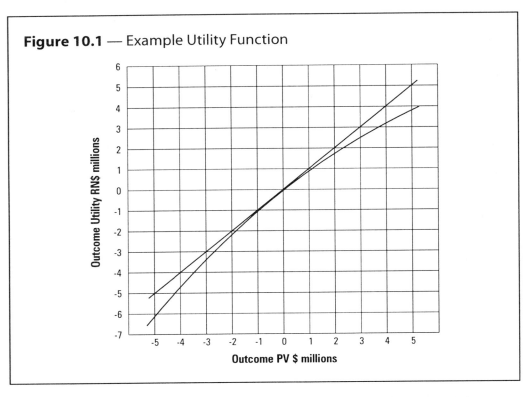

For small decisions, near zero PV, the straight line and the curve are nearly coincident. The result is that a value determined by EMV is nearly identical with the value obtained when recognizing risk-aversion.

Certainty Equivalent

An simple example will show how the utility function is used to make decisions. An EMV *decision tree* for the contract example is shown in Figure 10.2. The *objective* cost forecast and assessment is the EV of the possible outcomes. The cost-plus contract alternative at $1.3 million and the fixed-price contract alternatives have equal value to a *risk-neutral* decision maker. Recognizing a conservative risk policy requires a slight adjustment to the method.

Assume the company's *risk policy is the utility function* we saw in Figure 10.1. Some theorists suggest that this curve is appropriate to a company with a net worth of about $60 million. The degree of risk aversion is usually proportional to the size of the company. The risk tolerance coefficient typically used is one-fifth or one-sixth of the net worth of the organization. This is generally far too low for widely-held, public corporations.

To determine the fixed-price contract equivalent to the cost-plus contract uncertainty, first calculate the *expected utility* (EU) of the cost-plus contract. From the utility function [1]:

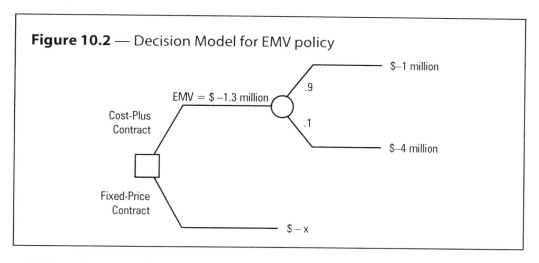

Figure 10.2 — Decision Model for EMV policy

Cost-Plus Contract

EMV = $ –1.3 million

.9 — $–1 million

.1 — $–4 million

Fixed-Price Contract

$ – x

U(-$1 million) = RN$-1.0517 million
U(-$4 million) = RN$-4.9182 million

Calculating EU, actually EV utility,

EU = .9(-1.0517) + .1(-4.9182)
     = RN$-1.4384 million.

The additional decimal places are shown to demonstrate the calculation method rather than to imply that tremendous precision is present.

EU is suited for comparing alternatives that all have uncertainties. Here, however, an uncertain alternative is being compared to a fixed outcome. *Dollars and utility cannot be compared* because of different units.

What we need to know is what guaranteed cost, $X is equivalent to the uncertain cost-plus alternative. $X represents what is called the ***certainty equivalent*** (CE).

The utility function is used to *translate EU into CE*. Figure 10.1 shows [2] that EU = RN$-1.4384 corresponds to a PV of $1.3439 million, the CE. For this company, a $1.3439 million fixed price contract is equivalent to the uncertain cost-plus contract.

Figure 10.3 shows a decision tree solution solved with the **expected utility decision policy.** The approximately $44,000 (=$1.3439 – 1.3 million) difference between CE and EMV is called the ***risk premium*** [3]. This premium is the additional amount the company is willing to pay, or sacrifice, to avoid risk. Note that CE and EMV are nearly the same in this case, even though the PV range is 30 percent of the scale. The risk premium is only 3.4 percent of the EMV.

Applying the Risk Policy

In decision analysis, alternatives are evaluated with either their EU's or CE's. The EMV decision policy is a special case: CE = EMV when the utility curve is a straight line [4]. Either EU or CE criterion results

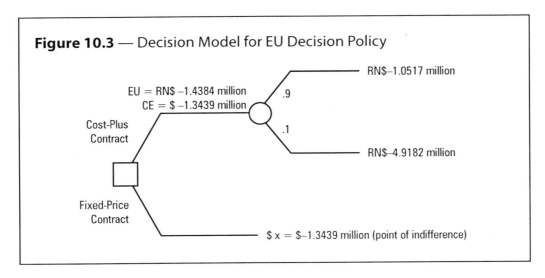

Figure 10.3 — Decision Model for EU Decision Policy

EU = RN$ –1.4384 million
CE = $ –1.3439 million

Cost-Plus
Contract

RN$–1.0517 million
.9

.1
RN$–4.9182 million

Fixed-Price
Contract

$ x = $–1.3439 million (point of indifference)

in the same decisions. However, if any alternative is a fixed dollar amount, conversion to CE's is necessary. When evaluating alternatives with utility it may be convenient to calculate every node's EMV, EU, and CE when back-solving decision trees. Costs along branches may then be subtracted from the CE's.

Interesting situations arise, sometimes, where the highest EMV alternative is not the same as the highest EU (or CE) alternative. That is the point of having a risk policy: to show which risk versus value trade-offs are appropriate.

An interesting application is in the problem of **optimizing participation** or working interest in a project. If the project has a positive EMV then the EMV decision rules says, "Take it all." However, if the potential downside is serious it may be advisable to share the risk with one or more partners. What is the optimal interest *you* would want in a project? *A utility function representing risk attitude is the logical way to solve this problem.* By iteration [5], deduce the shape of the function of EU (or CE) versus participation interest. Choose the participation interest that maximizes EU. Keeping 100 percent of the project is often desirable. However, if the project cost is high and there is sufficient risk, a fractional share of the project will maximize utility.

When running a Monte Carlo simulation, calculate the outcome value in PV, then convert to utility units. EU is the average of the utility-measured outcome.

When using Monte Carlo simulation, it is customary to provide the decision maker with risk versus value profile curves. These are typically cumulative probability distributions for PV and are the natural presentation format for simulation results. Most decision tree software provides similar, although stairstep-looking, graphs. Sample simulation-produced curves are shown in Figure 10.4.

When the curves cross *and* when the best-EMV alternative is riskier (wider), then risk policy is needed. It is an unfortunate reality that al-

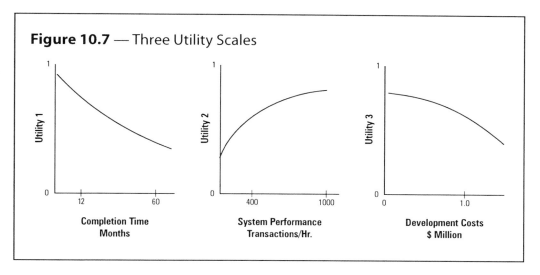

Figure 10.7 — Three Utility Scales

Completion Time
Months

System Performance
Transactions/Hr.

Development Costs
$ Million

Monte Carlo Solution

The project model simulation is run for each staffing alternative. On each trial, the completion time, system performance, and development cost are determined. These are converted to value components with the respective utility functions in Figure 10.7. The component utilities are combined with the weights assigned to each criterion. Arbitrarily, one might have component utilities use 0 to 1 scales and have the weighting fractions total 1; this ensures that the composite utility value function lies within a 0 to 1 range.

The Monte Carlo simulation model produced the following analysis results:

Normal Staffing: EU = 0.723
Fast-Track Staffing: EU = 0.693

Based on EU, the project manager logically chooses Normal Staffing. Figure 10.8 shows the three criteria distributions, and Figure 10.9 shows the composite value distribution. The EU's are sufficient to make a decision. The graphs provide supplemental information for the manager to check and to enhance his or her intuition about the project.

Summary

Project decisions are complicated when there are several objectives or sub-objectives. Three ways have been shown to structure decision policy in these cases. The starting point is always: be clear about the objectives. Decisions are easier if there is *focus on a single objective*. Consider these example single objectives:
• For corporations: Maximize shareholder value.
• For governments: Maximize the quality of life for citizens.

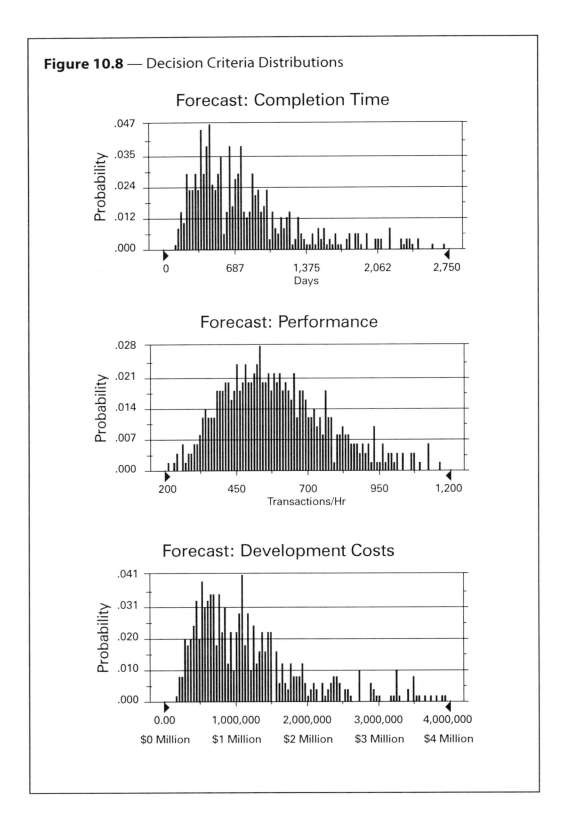

Figure 10.8 — Decision Criteria Distributions

Forecast: Completion Time

Forecast: Performance

Forecast: Development Costs

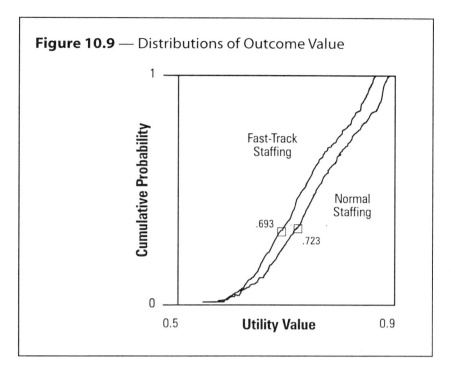

Figure 10.9 — Distributions of Outcome Value

- For professional associations: Maximize the organization's value to members.
- For individuals: Maximize personal ˈıappiness over a lifetime.

Measuring value toward the objective may have several components. Multiple criteria are sometimes used because it is inconvenient, or impossible, to fully develop the project model to assess value. Then we have a MCDM problem.

What causes *conflict*, is recognizing multiple objectives. Management should be clear about whose interests are being represented and what is to be optimized.

All approaches examined in this chapter employ a means to arrive at a *single* value measure for possible outcomes. Decision analysis explicitly recognizes risks with probabilities, which are used to weight possible outcomes. After applying probabilities, *we arrive at a single value for each alternative*. Using probabilities in this way is much better than recognizing "risk" as simply one more criterion.

Chapter Twelve

Summary and Recommendations

*Decision analysis helps people realize **faster, more confident decisions**. Uncertainties abound, and this general problem-solving approach explicitly incorporates judgments about uncertainties into the analysis.*

*The techniques are **applicable to all types of project decisions and valuations**. The feasibility study is often the first analysis of a project. Virtually all decisions involve committing resources, such as time and money. During construction or development there are many decisions to be made. Figure 12.1 illustrates the typical scope of project decisions. As the project advances, its forecast model can and should be updated as the situation moves from project management to operations to eventual abandonment.*

Retrospective

Previous chapters have described the approach and principal techniques of decision analysis.

There are no cookbooks. After constructing several decision analysis models, however, most people begin to see a pattern emerging. Typical analyses follow these steps:

- Determine the decision alternatives.
- For each alternative, identify the possible outcomes and the outcome values.
- Assess the probabilities (or distributions) for the various chance events.
- Solve for (usually) the expected monetary value [1] (EMV) for each alternative.
- Implement the best alternative.

This final chapter describes quick-and-dirty decision models; common errors in implementing decision analysis; strategies to help ensure success; mitigating and avoiding risks; and analysis tool selection.

Quick-and-Dirty Decisions

There is a common misconception that decision analysis is time-consuming. Many evaluations require only a few minutes with pencil, paper, and a hand calculator. Once you are clear about the best course of action—stop the analysis! No further value will be added.

Decisions that warrant more extensive analyses have one or more of these characteristics:

- Outcomes are difficult to value (requiring detailed cash flow modeling).
- Outcome values are significant for the entity and warrant serious attention to the decision.
- The best alternatives appear to have similar values or cost.
- There are too many variables, compounded by correlations, to process in one's head.

Common Simple Situation

Suppose you have created a base project plan. Upon further reflection, you now recognize a contingency that could affect project cost (and/or schedule). A simple tree-like model of this contingency is shown in Figure 12.2.

Brainstorming about the possibilities is an important project management function. Corporate planners call it S.W.O.T. analysis: identifying Strengths, Weaknesses, Opportunities and Threats. Note that contingencies can be either *unfavorable* (threats or *risks* [2]) or *favorable* (*opportunities*). A large project may have hundreds of identified risks and opportunities.

After a contingency has been identified, the manager should seek actions to exploit or mitigate the situation. This is where project management can be **proactive**, rather than waiting to become *reactive*. The actions may change the probability that the contingency event will occur; affect the project cost distribution (i.e., impact) should the contingency event occur; or affect *both* the probability and the impact of the contingency (least common).

Contingencies often can be met with several abatement (or exploitive) candidate actions. An action can preempt the contingency event. More often, actions result in only partial control. Flexibility and contingency plans are among the ways to reduce the impact of negative contingencies that do occur.

Following is a typical situation where a quick-and-dirty decision model is adequate.

Example. Suppose your project involves building several electromechanical instruments. Alignment is critical for certain components mounted on a base plate. The intended aluminum stock for fabricating the base plate is easy to work but may prove too-flexible and nondurable in the application.

Your team assesses a .12 chance that the planned aluminum base plate for fabrication will be inadequate. There are three upgrade alternatives shown in Table 12.1.

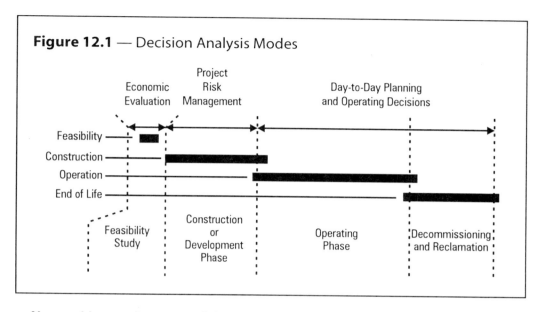

Figure 12.1 — Decision Analysis Modes

You could upgrade to one of these other choices now or see how the originally planned aluminum stock works out. Assume that if an initial base plate is not satisfactory, you will have sufficient information then to know what solution is required.

We can use Figure 12.2 as a template to express judgments about the risk and impact of the contingency. Figure 12.3 shows how the contingency could be appraised. The expected value (EV) cost of the contingency is $1,200. Whatever alternatives we consider must reduce the EV cost by more than the cost of implementing action. Decision analysts call this a *value of imperfect control* problem.

An Alternative. Your company can decide *now* to use thicker aluminum stock in the initial fabrication. This will cost $500 more initially. Is this prudent? Since the $500 is less than the $1,200 EV cost of plate inadequacy, the action alternative passes the first feasibility test.

Figure 12.4 shows the decision model. You want to evaluate whether this conservative approach is a justifiable precaution.

The thicker base plate reduces [3] the contingency probability from .12 to .072. If it is inadequate, then the probability that Premium Stock is needed increases from .50 to .833. Similarly, the probability of Need Casting increases from .10 to .167. In this case, the candidate action (Thicker Stock Initially) affects *both* the probability and the impact of the contingency.

The EV cost of refabrication drops from $1,200 to $960 when the thicker plate is used initially. However, the case with the thicker plate costs $500. Thus the comparable EV cost of with the thicker plate initially is $1,460. Therefore, *choosing Planned Aluminum Stock is most appropriate* (for a risk-neutral decision maker or an organization that has an EMV policy). The Thicker Stock Initially is a worse option, having a $260 higher EV cost.

Summary and Recommendations

Figure 12.2 — Simple Contingency Template

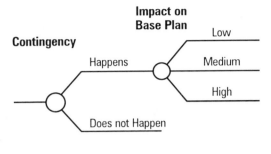

Table 12.1 — Improved Base Plate Material

Upgrade to	Probability* of Being Adequate	Cost ** to Rebuild
Thicker Stock	.40	$5,000
Premium Grade Stock (but more difficult to machine)	.90	$10,000
Machined Casting	1.00	$30,000

*Conditional given that the original stock and fabrication prove inadequate.

**Include monetary-equivalent penalties for project delay.

Thus we obtain a logical, defensible basis for the decision. This type of quick-and-dirty decision analysis fits many situations and should be in every project manager's tool kit.

Common Implementation Errors

The author has been fortunate, on occasion, to assist clients with rationalizing their evaluation practices and decision policy. Some frequently observed shortcomings include:

- Confusion about the company's decision policy. Often, there are unvoiced criteria and hurdles [4].
- Using decision criteria that do not correspond directly to the company's objective.
- Using higher hurdles in an effort to establish a conservative risk policy. A better approach for conservatism is to establish a company's utility function.
- Not assessing *incremental* project value. A common error, for example, is including fixed costs in a project evaluation.

- Low risk: reasonably assured volumes, costs, and prices
- Preliminary evaluation
- Doing a base-case evaluation or sensitivity analysis
- Clear choice of the best alternative (perhaps the analysis forecast is only for a budget plan).

Stochastic Models. People often ask: Which tool is better—decision trees or Monte Carlo simulation? The answer depends upon the problem. Neither technique is inherently superior. However, each technique is better at solving certain problems.

Table 12.2 lists decision situation attributes vs. tool. Check marks show, with all other things equal, whether decision tree analysis or Monte Carlo simulation would be preferred. There are a few other calculation methods, usually for special situations, but trees and simulation remain the workhorses of decision analysis.

Summary

What are the characteristics of successful executives? Of successful professionals? Surveys consistently show **decision-making ability** at or near the top of the lists. Perhaps no activity is more important. Surprisingly little training investment is made toward developing this important skill.

Most decisions are about resource allocation: where do we put our time, money and other resources so that they will do us the most good? That is what decision analysis is about.

Probability is the **language of uncertainty**. Decision analysis provides the only logical, consistent way to incorporate judgments about uncertainties into an analysis. Expected value is perhaps the most powerful management concept since the invention of the organization hierarchy.

Good decisions increase the likelihood of, but do not guarantee, good outcomes. However, making good decisions over the long term maximizes the likelihood of good progress toward the organization's objective. People who use decision analysis can sleep well at night knowing that they have made the best possible choices under the circumstances.

There is a ***strong bias for action***. There is no reason to delay—unless "Delay" is the best alternative in your analysis. Often a ten-minute, quick-and-dirty calculation is sufficient to see whether a decision can be made now.

Central to the decision analysis approach are:
- *Value function*. This measures "goodness" toward the organization's objective(s). For most purposes, dollars are a suitable measure (non-monetary objectives can be translated into dollar-equivalents). Alternatively, multi-criteria *value functions* translate several important facets of a problem into a single value measure.

- *Probability distributions.* These express judgments about risks and uncertainties. Distributions are used in calculations and can be used also in presenting the results of a decision analysis.
- *Expected value.* This is how risk and value are combined for making decisions. Maximizing expected monetary value (EMV) expresses a complete, succinct decision policy appropriate for many organizations.

The concepts are straightforward once you know about them. The methodology is proven and accessible. With practice, decision analysis is easily integrated into the professional's everyday problem-solving.

Endnotes

Chapter 2

1. *Optimizing* can address the best compromise across multiple criteria. *Optimizing* and *maximizing* are equivalent terms when we have a single value (objective) function.

2. For public, widely-held corporations the author recommends designing decision policy so that project evaluations represent incremental shareholder value. The cost of equity component should be the rate stockholders would demand for a nearly risk-free investment of similar duration. A home mortgage with a term similar to the project may be a reasonable approximation to the typical investor's marginal cost of risk-free capital. For projects highly correlated to the capital markets, the discount rate should be slightly higher.

3. A better perspective might be the typical stockholder's net worth times the number of stockholders. For a discussion see Schuyler, John R., 1995, "Rational Is Practical Better Evaluations through the Logic of Shareholder Value," *Proceedings,* SPE Hydrocarbon Economics and Evaluation Symposium, March 17–28, Dallas, pp. 323–336, Society of Petroleum Engineers' paper no. 030066.

Chapter 4

1. An excellent source of inspiration in creating and evaluating alternatives is: Keeney, Ralph L. 1992. *Value-Focused Thinking: A Path to Creative Decisionmaking.* Harvard University Press, Cambridge, Massachusetts, 416 p. This book is about multi-criteria decision making.

2. The second nodes are judgments about the *quality of the information.* The first node is the *prior probability* assessments about the event that matters. Figure 3 has nodes in inverse sequence from that needed in the decision model. However, eliciting the judgments in this manner separates them so that the expert(s) need consider only one event at a time.

Chapter 5

1. This is *conventional* Monte Carlo sampling for independent variables. There are other Monte Carlo sampling methods available.

2. Technically, this is a reverse cumulative **frequency** distribution. "Frequency" refers to sample data, in this case, simulation trials. A frequency distribution converges to the true probability density distribution if collected in many fine bins and after sufficient trials. This chapter refers to the simulation outputs also as probability distributions.

3. The accuracy of the $96,000 EMV *improvement* (over Skid Now) is ±$4.2k, measured by a statistic called *standard error of the mean* $\sigma_{\bar{x}} = \frac{s}{\sqrt{n}}$, where s is the standard deviation of the outcome value and n is the number of trials. We know the error function is normally distributed from the *central limit theorem*. Thus, there is about a .68 probability that the true EV, approached after many more trials, will lie in the range of $\bar{x} \pm \sigma_{\bar{x}}$. That is, a 68% confidence interval for the true EMV solution is the range $91.8k to $100.2k. Halving the EV estimate uncertainty requires quadrupling the number of simulation trials. The 1000-trial simulation requires 46 seconds on a Pentium 133 PC running Microsoft QuickBASIC 4.5 in interpreter mode (rather than compiled) under Windows 95.

4. The bimodal (two-peak) distribution is a common shape of the distribution of net improvement between alternatives in a project model. This feature arises because of the stochastic nature of the critical path.

Chapter 6

1. See, for example, Kelly, J.E., and Morgan R. Walker. 1959. Critical Path Planning and Scheduling. *Proceedings*, Eastern Joint Computer Conference, Boston, Dec. 1-3, 1959, 160-173. For a more recent description of the development of the capabilities of CPPS, see Kelly, James, Jr. and Morgan R. Walker. 1989. The Origins of CPM: A Personal History. *PM Network*, vol. III, no. 2, February, 7-22.

2. Malcolm, D.G., J.H. Rosenboom, and G.E. Clark. 1959. Application of a Technique for Research and Development Program Evaluation. *Operations Research*, vol. 7, 646-69.

3. Some people have added correlation between variables to PERT, but this is difficult except with simple relationships and distributions.

4. See Santell, M.P., J.R. Jung, Jr., and J.C. Warner. 1992. Optimization in Project Coordination Scheduling Through Application of Taguchi Methods. *Project Management Journal*, vol. 23, no. 3 (Sept.), 5-15. Warner wrote a contemporaneous three-part tutorial in *PM Network*: Part I, May 1992, 36-40; Part II, July 1992, 34-38; Part III, August 1992, 69-74.

5. Juran, J.M. and Frank M. Gryna, Jr. 1980. *Quality Planning and Analysis: From Product Development Through Use.* 2nd ed. McGraw-Hill. 208.

6. The next higher moments include *skewness* (third moment about the mean/σ^3) and *kurtosis* (= fourth moment about the mean/σ^4). Skewness measures the extent of asymmetry (0 is symmetric). Kurtosis measures peakedness (a normal distribution has a kurtosis of 3). Higher moments are useful in more fully describing the distribution shape; this is especially important when working with distribution tails.

7. The weighted center of a probability distribution is the balance point about which the torque is zero. The EV is the probability graph's center of gravity projected to the x-axis.

8. Typically, PERT uses activity times estimated by a Low, Most Likely and High. This approximately specifies a *beta distribution* with the statistics

$$\mu = \frac{\text{Low} + 4(\text{Most Likely}) + \text{High}}{6} \text{ and } \sigma = \frac{\text{High} - \text{Low}}{6}.$$

decision tree

a graphical representation of a decision problem and the expected value calculations, consisting of decision, chance and terminal nodes connected by branches.

delta property

feature of *expected value* such that a constant amount added to each outcome increases the EV by that amount.

dependence or dependency

when the outcome of one chance event influences, or is influenced by, the outcome of another chance event. Dependent relationships are often represented by formula relationships or with correlation coefficients.

deterministic

said of a model where all parameters are fixed or "determinate."

discount rate

the "interest" rate used for present value discounting.

discounted cash flow analysis

projecting a future cash flow stream and determining its present value.

discounting cash flow (DCF)

the sum of individual yearly cash flow amounts which have been multiplied by the appropriate present value discount factors.

discounted cash flow rate of return (DCF-ROR)

same as "internal rate of return."

discounted return on investment (DROI or DCF-ROI)

ratio of PV/PV (investment). Popular as a ranking criterion for capital constrained decision making.

discrete event or distribution

a chance event that as a finite number of outcomes. Cf. *continuous event*.

discrete event simulation

Monte Carlo simulation where the emphasis is on state changes of objects within the system. The clock advances to the next event. Cf. *continuous event simulation*.

evaluation

general term for any type of analysis used for asset appraisal, feasibility study, engineering evaluation, project assessment, and all other types of analyses related to decisions.

expected monetary value (EMV)

Expected value of a measurement expressed in monetary terms. Usually refers to the expected value of present value, E(PV) or EV PV.

expected value (EV)

probability weighted average of all possible outcomes. When the outcomes are measured in monetary units, the term is usually called *expected monetary value* (EMV).

forecast

a judged or predicted view of the event sequence or future state of the world. A forecast is the best *projection*. See *projection*.

fuzzy logic

rules of logic based on the idea that events can be classified by degree of membership. For example, a qualitative assessment, such as "high cost," can be quantified and used in logical calculations.

Gaussian distribution

see *normal distribution*.

general and administrative expense (G&A)

company overhead not directly attributed to operations.

good decision

one that is logical and consistent with the values of the decision maker and all of the data available at the time.

histogram

graph showing frequency of observations counted in segments of the value range. Often presented as a bar chart.

independence

the characteristic where one event does not affect the occurrence of another, and vice versa.

influence diagram

network diagram of system variables with arcs indicating the direction of "influence" or time-sequenced relationships. Variables and formulas can be quantified and expected values solved by an iterative process as an alternative to decision tree calculations.

internal rate of return (IRR)

a discount rate that yields a *present value*=0. There may be multiple roots when the cumulative net cashflow curve changes sign more than once. Calculating IRR requires an iterative, trial-and-error procedure. Synonymous with *rate of return* (ROR) and *discounted cash flow rate of return* (DCF-ROR).

joint probability

the probability of two or more events occurring together. Intersection of two sets, such as represented in a Venn diagram.

judgment

a probability distribution assessment performed, at least in part, by a human. *Subjective probability* assessment.

mean

the arithmetic average of equally-likely outcomes or a set of observations. The probability-weighted average. This is usually the best estimator for a chance event. Synonymous with *expected value* when referring to the mean of a *probability density distribution*.

median

the most central value of a population or sample set. Half of the other values lie above, and the other half below. With an even number of equally likely outcomes or observations, the median is the average of the two center-most values.

merge bias

the EV start time of a project activity is later than the maximum EV finish time of predecessor activities. This effect occurs at the joining or merging of arcs, moving left to right, in a project (activity) network diagram.

mitigate

to eliminate or lessen the risk or effect of, e.g., mitigate the impact of bad weather.

mode

the particular outcome that is most likely. This is the highest point on a probability density distribution curve. A curve with two localized maxima is called *bimodal*. With frequency *histogram* data, the mode is typically the midpoint of the bin having the most counts.